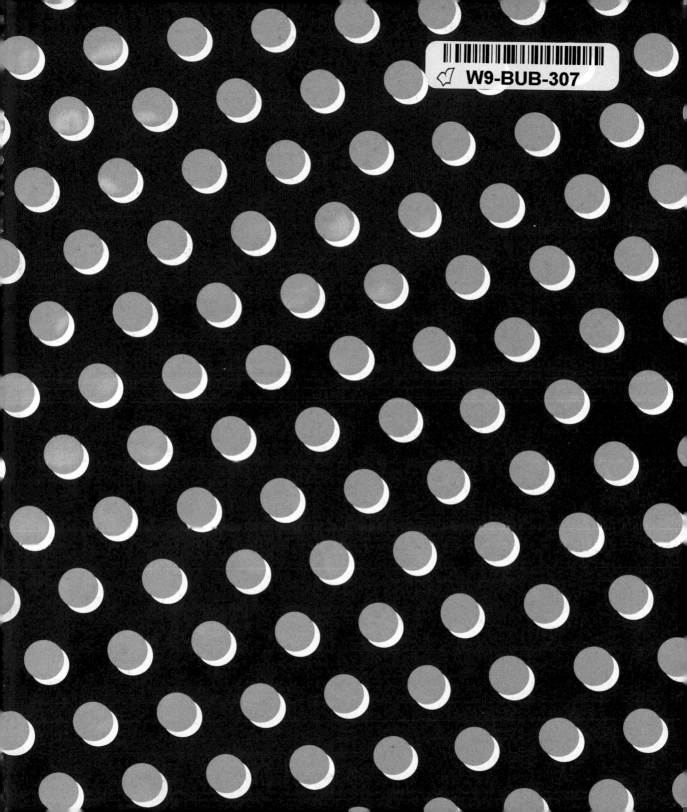

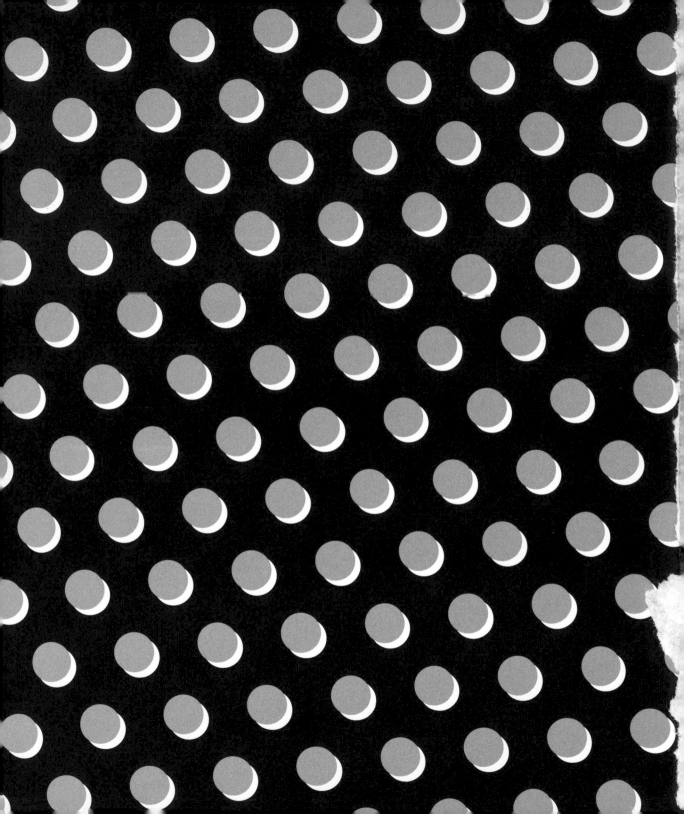

HOW OLD AM I?

Phaidon Press Limited
2 Cooperage Yard
London E15 2QR

Phaidon Press Inc.
65 Bleecker Street
New York, NY 10012

phaidon.com

First published 2021
Copyright © 2021 Phaidon Press Limited
Text and Concept © Julie Pugeat
Project and Artworks © JR

Typeset in Circular Pro and Plaak 4

ISBN 978 1 83866 158 8
013-0121

Edited by Maya Gartner
Designed by Meagan Bennett
Production by Rebecca Price

Printed in Italy

JR · INSIDE OUT PROJECT

HOW OLD AM I?

1 ●━━━━━━━━━━━━➤ 100

FACES FROM AROUND THE WORLD

Φ

WHERE DO YOU LIVE?

WHERE WERE YOU BORN?

WHAT MAKES YOU HAPPY?

WHAT IS YOUR WISH FOR THE WORLD?

NO MATTER HOW OLD WE ARE OR WHERE WE LIVE,

WE EACH HAVE A STORY TO TELL.

WHAT'S YOURS?

HELLO! MY NAME IS GWEN.

I AM **1** YEAR OLD.

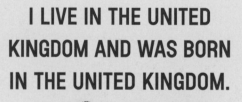

I LIVE IN THE UNITED KINGDOM AND WAS BORN IN THE UNITED KINGDOM.

Now that I am 1, I can say some words and pick out picture books that I love having my parents read to me. I can also crawl really fast and almost walk. The things that make me happy are milk, music, laughter, and my family. I'm curious about everything!

¡HOLA! MY NAME IS LORENZO.

I AM  2 YEARS OLD.

I LIVE IN MEXICO AND WAS BORN IN MEXICO.

For my next birthday, I want a party with my friends, presents, and a piñata. Eating makes me happy. When I grow up, I want to be like my dad.

HELLO! MY NAME IS LUKA.

I AM **3** YEARS OLD.

I LIVE IN BARBADOS AND WAS BORN IN BARBADOS.

I am looking forward to my next birthday. I'm going to be 4 years old, and that makes me really happy. When I get older, I want to be ME. My dad always makes me happy!

SALAMA! MY NAME IS SAHÈL HAVRAN.

I AM 4 YEARS OLD.

I LIVE IN MADAGASCAR AND WAS BORN IN MADAGASCAR.

I would love a toy car for my 5th birthday. I'm really proud to be able to go to the bathroom by myself at night. Eating cakes and playing makes me happy. When I'm 26 years old, I want to be a train driver or a doctor for children. When I get older, I want to fill the world with a lot of big buildings!

HEJ! MY NAME IS ELSA.

I AM  YEARS OLD.

I LIVE IN SWEDEN AND WAS BORN IN SWEDEN.

I can't wait for my next birthday. I'm having a party! I like surprises, especially on my birthday. When I'm 30, I would love to be a princess. My name is Elsa, so I will be Princess Elsa. Being with my friends and eating ice cream makes me happy. I wish for the world to be completely glittery and shiny.

BONJOUR! MY NAME IS NOAM.

I AM  **6** YEARS OLD.

I LIVE IN THE USA AND WAS BORN IN FRANCE.

I am super excited about my next birthday – I wish it was today! I am proud because I already know how to read, dance, and go to sleepovers. When I'm 18, I want to be the President of America. Chocolate is what makes me happy. I wish the whole world was made of chocolate and that when you want to eat some chocolate, you can just take it from the walls around you. Chocolate is what makes everybody happy.

SAT SRI AKAL! MY NAME IS RANIA.

I AM **7** YEARS OLD.

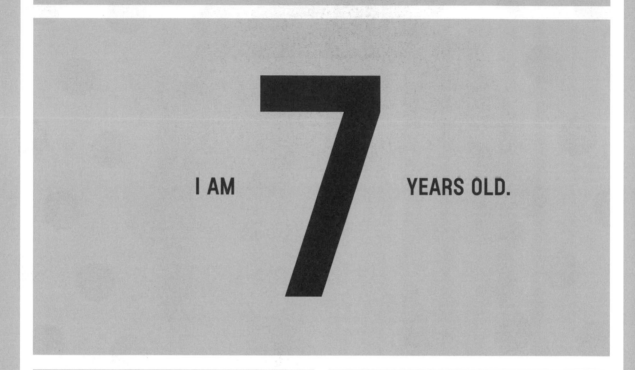

I LIVE IN THE USA AND WAS BORN IN INDIA.

It's fun to be 7. I'm braver than before because it's easier to make new friends. It's also kind of hard sometimes because other kids act as if they were older, like when boys and girls like each other. When I'm 30, I want to be a teacher. My family and pets are what make me happy. I wish for happiness and no homework for everyone in the world.

CIAO! MY NAME IS OLIVIA.

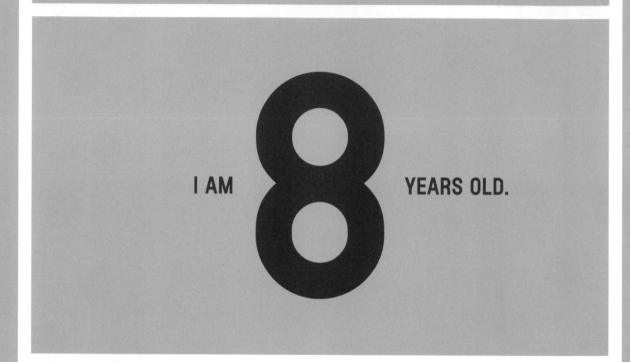

I AM **8** YEARS OLD.

I LIVE IN ITALY AND WAS BORN IN ITALY.

I wish to go back in time and be a 6-month-old baby. I don't remember what it was like to be that age, and I want to know how it feels. I also wish to be 30, so I can cook alone, drive a car, and have my own cat. It makes me happy to take cold showers when it's hot and hot showers when it's cold. I wish the world had a single language, so children of all countries could talk to each other easily.

NǏ HǍO! MY NAME IS ANAN.

I AM **9** YEARS OLD.

I LIVE IN CHINA AND WAS BORN IN CHINA.

There is a virus going around right now and I don't get to play outside too much, so I like to play just outside of my apartment. I am looking forward to being 11 because I really like swimming, and swimming classes start when you are 11 at my school. I think the best ages are 27 and 30 because by then, my dream to become a dancer will come true!

¡HOLA! MY NAME IS DIEGO.

I AM

10

YEARS OLD.

I LIVE IN COSTA RICA AND WAS BORN IN COSTA RICA.

Some people say that I'm not a child anymore, but I still think I am. Being a child is great because I can do all the things that kids like to do. My best age was when I was 3 because I wasn't quite a big kid but also wasn't a baby anymore. What makes me happy is when I spend time with my family or friends and when we give love and receive it back.

BONJOUR! MY NAME IS JOHNSON.

I AM 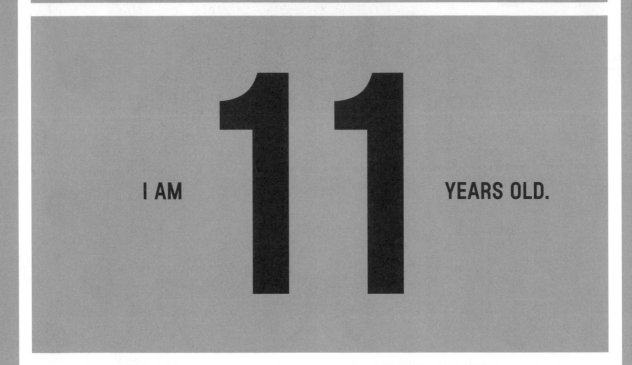 **11** YEARS OLD.

I LIVE IN FRANCE AND WAS BORN IN HAITI.

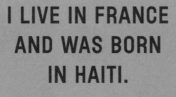

I feel grown up because I've just changed schools. It feels like a new life! I don't think I want to be 80 because I may not be able to mountain bike anymore, which I love. When I am 18, I would like to be a pizza maker at the pizza restaurant in my village. They make the best pizza in the world! I wish for the world to be free of pollution and for Earth to never be destroyed.

SELAM! MY NAME IS AMIRA.

I AM 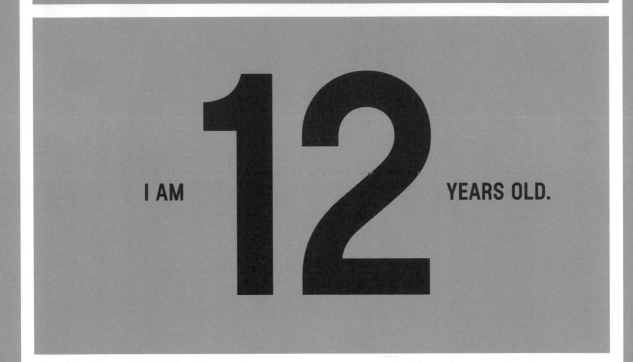 **12** YEARS OLD.

I LIVE IN THE USA AND WAS BORN IN ETHIOPIA.

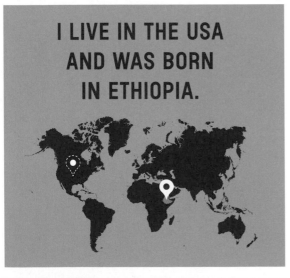

At my age, it feels like you are in between a kid and a teenager. I feel scared about becoming a teenager as I will have things I must do and may not have as much time to have fun. I would like to become a dancer in a dance company. I will be able to do this when I am 21. I wish for people to take better care of the environment. We need a healthy planet for everyone.

DOBRY DEN! MY NAME IS TOMA.

I AM **13** YEARS OLD.

I LIVE IN BULGARIA AND WAS BORN IN BULGARIA.

My dream and goal for as long as I can remember has been to become an actor. The most important things in my life are my family and friends. My wish for the world is that we all take care of nature and animals. I also wish that we all be kind to each other. I think these things will change the world in a good way.

HALLO! MY NAME IS OSCAR.

I AM **14** YEARS OLD.

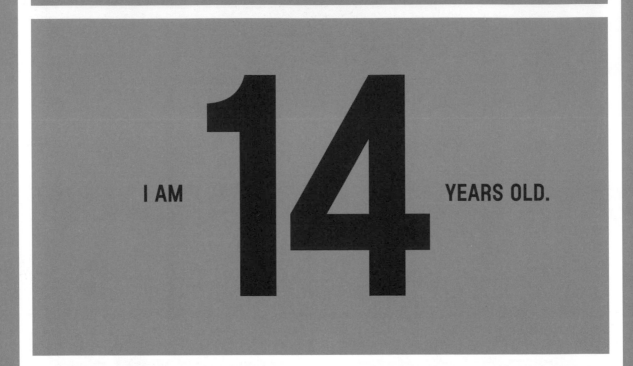

I LIVE IN NORWAY AND WAS BORN IN NORWAY.

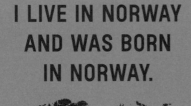

I love my family, my friends, my dog Jay, and going to school. I like living in Norway. I live very close to the forest and a cross-country ski track that goes along flat ground, so I can go skiing at any time. I do this many times a week! I want to be a doctor when I grow up because I really like helping other people. I was 11 when I first thought of becoming a doctor.

KUMUSTA! MY NAME IS JUSTIN.

I AM **15** YEARS OLD.

I LIVE IN FRANCE AND WAS BORN IN THE PHILIPPINES.

Since I was 11 years old, my dream has been to join the Paris firefighter brigade as a firefighter one day. I had to wait three years to be old enough to join my local junior firefighter group. They are called a squad. I spend every Wednesday afternoon with them. I want to learn as much as I can to help those around me. My wish for the world is that all countries agree to stop the destruction of forests and protect all our animals.

¡HOLA! MY NAME IS LIAM.

I AM **16** YEARS OLD.

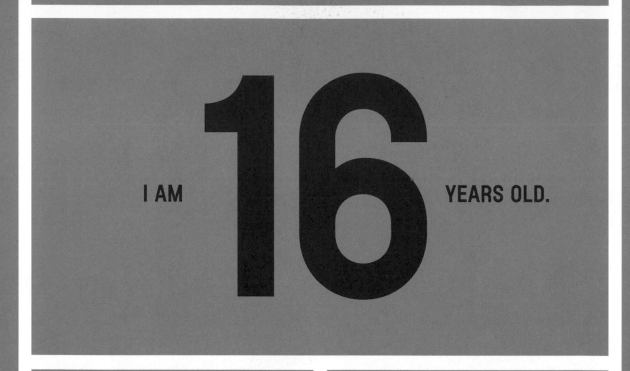

I LIVE IN URUGUAY AND WAS BORN IN URUGUAY.

I am 16, but I feel like I'm 20 years old. I study art and I am happy to be who I am. I was born as a girl, but I have always known I was a boy. I am looking forward to turning 18, so that I can have my first operation to become a boy. It is something that is very important to me. The most important thing for ourselves and our surroundings is peace and, above all, love.

BONJOUR! MY NAME IS DARIA.

I AM **17** YEARS OLD.

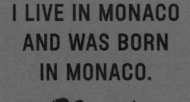

I LIVE IN MONACO AND WAS BORN IN MONACO.

Being 17 is so much fun, but I also feel a lot of pressure because I am expected to be an adult. I am very excited about turning 18. A huge part of my life is ending because I will be finishing school, but also a whole new adventure will begin! What matters to me is meeting and sharing experiences with other people and the chance to travel and study. I hope that I can be helpful to others in my life.

BONJOUR! MY NAME IS SASHA.

I AM **18** YEARS OLD.

I LIVE IN SWITZERLAND AND WAS BORN IN SWITZERLAND.

In my country you are considered an adult when you turn 18, so I am now a grown-up! I'm just at the very beginning of my life and there is so much for me to do. I want to discover the world, find love, and have an interesting job. But to have these things, I must first finish studying, which is my main goal right now. I'm going to study engineering (how to design and make the useful things around us, like buildings and machines) in college.

SALAM! MY NAME IS MATIN.

I AM 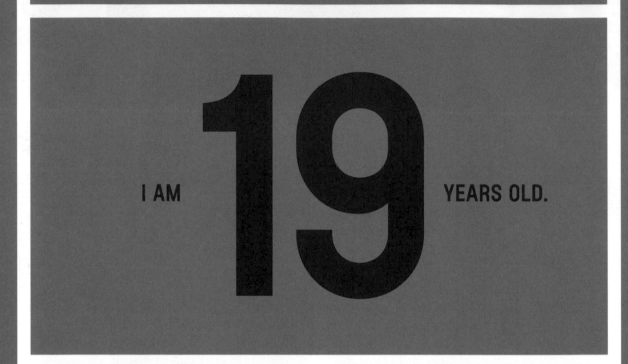 19 YEARS OLD.

I LIVE IN IRAN AND WAS BORN IN IRAN.

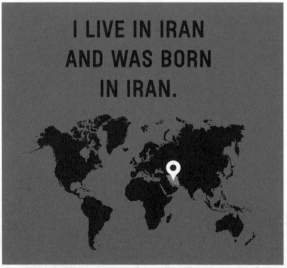

I'm a student and a photographer. Simple things in life, like books or flowers, make me happy. It's also very important for me to help the people around me. I want the world to be a place of peace and freedom. I would like all children to have free education and science learning.

¡HOLA! MY NAME IS PAMELA.

I AM **20** YEARS OLD.

I LIVE IN PARAGUAY AND WAS BORN IN PARAGUAY.

I like being 20. I think I'll enjoy being 21 as well. A lot can happen in a year! I remember being 11 as special because that was when my father told us that we were moving to another city. I felt scared but also excited because my grandparents, uncles, aunts, and cousins were already living there. It was also the same year that my country got really close to winning the World Cup in soccer! I was so happy!

SALAM! MY NAME IS AMAARAH.

I AM **21** YEARS OLD.

I LIVE IN SOUTH AFRICA AND WAS BORN IN SOUTH AFRICA.

The most important age for me was 19 because that was when I started college. But being 21 is exciting as well because it feels like the beginning of being an adult. I'm looking forward to being 35 because it seems like you have a lot of strength, love, and life experience at that age. My life has taught me that at any age you can decide to be a good person who spreads happiness.

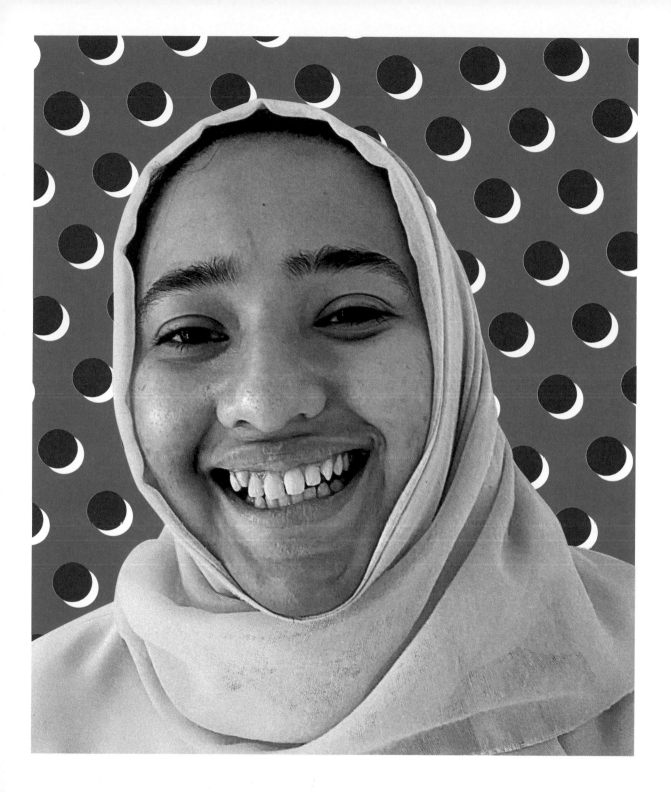

SALAM! MY NAME IS MOHAMAD.

I AM **22** YEARS OLD.

I LIVE IN LEBANON AND WAS BORN IN LEBANON.

I have always loved cars. When I was 8, my uncle's car broke down, but somehow I knew what the problem was and I solved it! I was young, but I think my curiosity and wanting to learn about how things work helped me. When I was 13, I really started to read a lot about cars. Then, in high school, I decided that I wanted to study engineering to be able to work on designing and building my own cars!

GRÜß DICH! MY NAME IS MICHAELA.

I AM **23** YEARS OLD.

I LIVE IN AUSTRIA
AND WAS BORN
IN AUSTRIA.

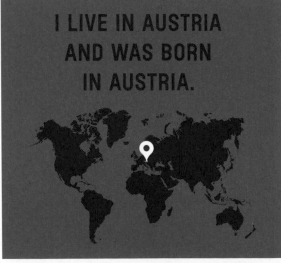

I feel good about my age – I am not too young or too old. Being 16 was important for me because I felt old enough to make my own decisions but still young enough to make mistakes. My favorite age is 18 because a lot of things happen – you finish high school, you decide what you want to do, and you feel a little bit more free. I love to get people to smile and be happy.

HELLÓ! MY NAME IS KLAUDIA.

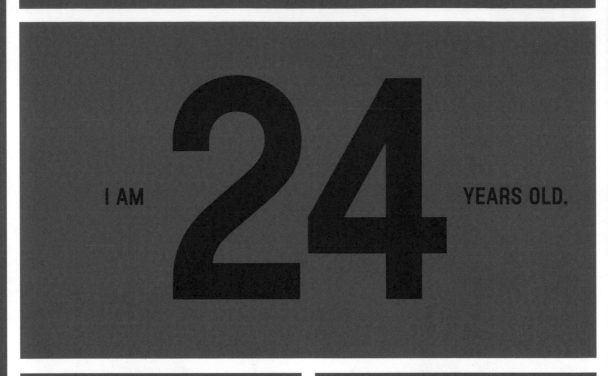

I AM **24** YEARS OLD.

I LIVE IN SPAIN AND WAS BORN IN HUNGARY.

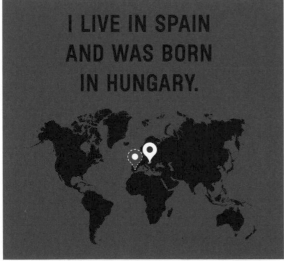

When I was 20, I decided to move from Budapest in Hungary to Madrid in Spain to start a new life as an "adult." This was a very big step for me. I'm a teacher now, and I like working with kids and learning new languages. For me, taking care of yourself is really important. We have to learn about ourselves and know what makes us happy. Being with family and friends makes me happy, as does playing sports, especially karate.

MARHABA! MY NAME IS ASMAA.

I AM **25** YEARS OLD.

I LIVE IN THE USA AND WAS BORN IN SYRIA.

When I was 8, my parents put me in a dance class to give me confidence. After my first class, I believed I could do anything! I love my age. I feel like Superwoman, and I'm not afraid to grow up some more. I loved being 10 because I ate a lot of ice cream. Now I am an architectural designer who draws buildings. I love creating buildings that people can live in. I think it's important to create things that bring people together.

HEI! MY NAME IS KALLE.

I AM **26** YEARS OLD.

I LIVE IN FINLAND AND WAS BORN IN FINLAND.

I was about 8 when I started to explore the forests and fields near my home with my friends and brother and sisters. I still remember all the secret paths through the forests and the trees and boulders I knew. When I was 19, I met a girl. Seven years later, we live together, and she is the most important person in my life. The most valuable thing in the world is the people you love and trust. I am grateful I have so many wonderful people around me.

JAMBO! MY NAME IS ESTHER.

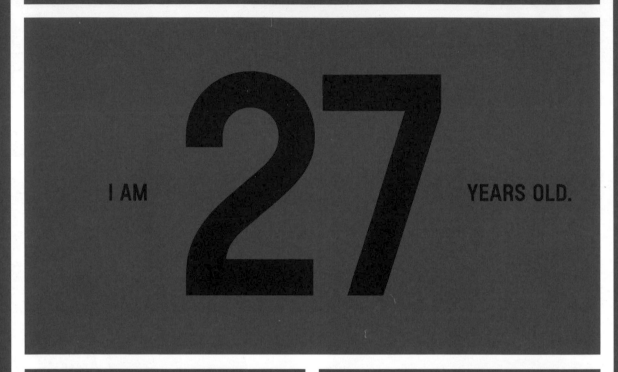

I AM **27** YEARS OLD.

I LIVE IN THE USA AND WAS BORN IN KENYA.

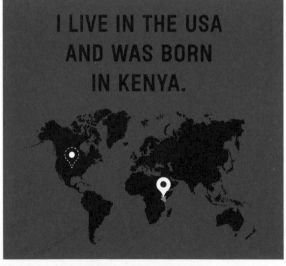

Growing up on a farm taught me how to be helpful and kind to others. I always helped with getting food from the garden, cleaning the house, and taking care of the animals. Now I am grown up and have become a designer, someone who makes things that are easy and fun to use. But I still do my best to care for others wherever I go. I think age is just a number that helps tell your story – it does not say who you are.

SELAMAT PAGI! MY NAME IS SHEENA.

I AM **28** YEARS OLD.

I LIVE IN MALAYSIA AND WAS BORN IN MALAYSIA.

When I was 12, I started acting for TV. It was very fun but hard work! When I was 15 I became a model. I had my pictures taken for magazines and websites. I waited until I finished college before I started modeling jobs in big cities like London, Paris, and Milan. I still do it now! When a friend says something kind to me, it makes me happy. Words have the power to build people up. It's important to tell your friends to follow their dreams.

SVEIKI! MY NAME IS SOLVEIGA.

I AM **29** YEARS OLD.

I LIVE IN LATVIA AND WAS BORN IN LATVIA.

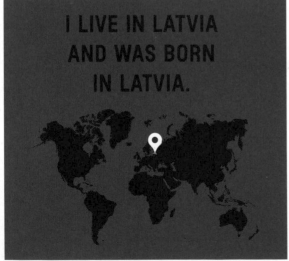

When I was a kid, I used to collect stones from all the places I visited with my family. I wanted to be a geologist who explored the world through minerals and rocks. Now I am a photographer who explores the world through a camera lens, but I still bring stones back to remind me of the places I've been. I hope I inspire others to look for adventures too. I wish for everyone to see the beauty in everything around us.

HELLO! MY NAME IS KEVIN.

I AM **30** YEARS OLD.

I LIVE IN NIGERIA AND WAS BORN IN NIGERIA.

When I was 6, I found my mother's old cameras. I was amazed to discover the world through them, and I took pictures of everything I saw. I didn't realize it at the time, but this was the first thing that made me want to become a photographer. When I was 12, I wanted to be a Formula 1 car racer. But sometimes life doesn't turn out like we'd planned, and I am happy with that. I'm looking forward to eating cake on my next birthday!

OLÁ! MY NAME IS NADEILEN.

I AM **31** YEARS OLD.

I LIVE IN BELGIUM AND WAS BORN IN THE REPUBLIC OF CABO VERDE.

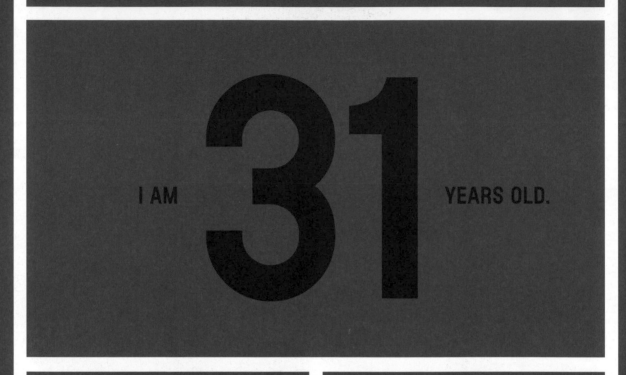

Being 31 is cool because I can do whatever I want – even silly things like drawing cartoons, eating too many cookies, or playing with a balloon – and still be an adult. I am not in a hurry to grow up, but when I do grow up, I want to be more creative. Making other people happy is what makes me happy and my wish for the world is that we all treat each other the way we want to be treated.

TERE! MY NAME IS LIISI.

I AM **32** YEARS OLD.

I LIVE IN ESTONIA AND WAS BORN IN ESTONIA.

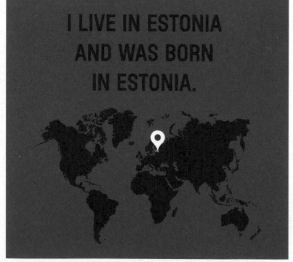

Sometimes I think it's too late to learn something new, like a language or a musical instrument. But my 91-year-old grandmother, Lilli, inspires me to think differently. She began to use a computer when she was 80! When she was little, she went to school on a horse and never had computers or the Internet. I hope to be like her when I am 91. She is still curious and ready to try new things. Maybe I will inspire my own grandchildren one day!

MHORO! MY NAME IS NGONIDZASHE.

I AM  **33** YEARS OLD.

I LIVE IN ZIMBABWE AND WAS BORN IN ZIMBABWE.

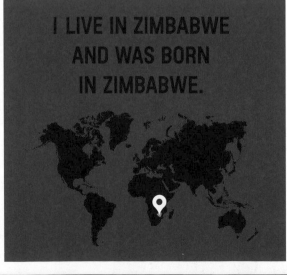

When I was a kid, I had questions about everything. I was about 8 when I knew that I wanted to spend my life learning and discovering things. When I got older, I worked out how to use a camera. I took pictures of music concerts, friends, and cities – and the camera became my key to exploring the world. I am 33 now and still asking a lot of questions, but I have my camera and my curiosity to help me answer them!

I AM

34

YEARS OLD.

I LIVE IN RUSSIA
AND WAS BORN
IN RUSSIA.

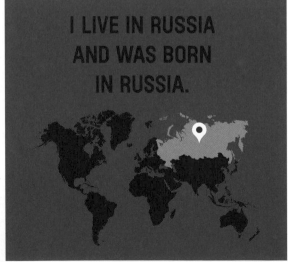

When I was little I thought anything
was possible. I still believe this now!
When I was around 5 to 8, I had
a wild imagination. I could be a
princess one day, or a firefighter
or teacher another. I'm still interested
in different lives and now have a job
making documentaries – movies that
show the world around us and the
lives of real people. I learn about all
kinds of people in different places –
from Tokyo to California, from
Norway to Madagascar.

NĬ HÀO! MY NAME IS GRACE.

I AM  YEARS OLD.

I LIVE IN HONG KONG AND WAS BORN IN HONG KONG.

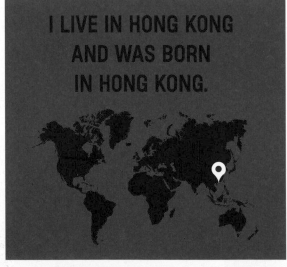

When I was 6, I used to have a lot of time alone. I created my own world at home, turning the living room into an imaginary forest. I doodled my dreams on the side that is underneath our dining table every day for four years. I only got caught when we decided to move to another apartment and the house movers flipped over the table. The grand review of my secret masterpiece was a really proud moment.

¡HOLA! MY NAME IS FRANCISCO.

I AM **36** YEARS OLD.

I LIVE IN PANAMÁ AND WAS BORN IN PANAMÁ.

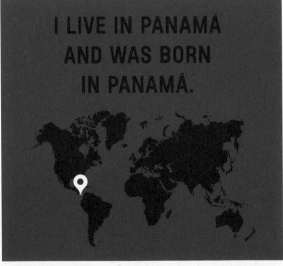

I feel amazing about my age because I learn new things about myself every day. When I was 29, I realized that I was meant to be an actor. Now I am an actor and a singer. When I was younger, I didn't know what I wanted to be. But I thought big and did everything I could to make those dreams come true. It always makes me happy when I go to bed at night knowing that I did my best that day.

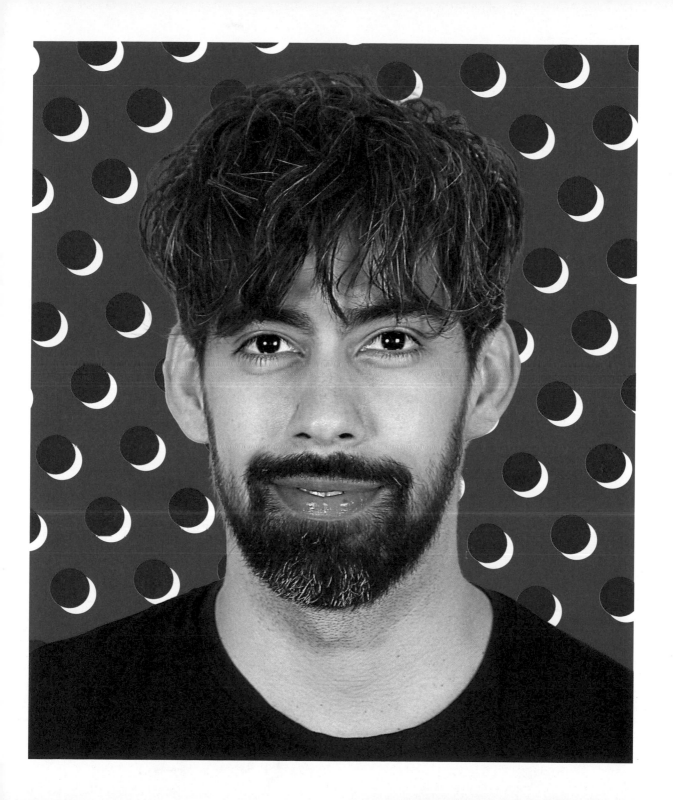

SALAM! MY NAME IS ABEDARAHMAN.

I AM  **37** YEARS OLD.

I LIVE IN PALESTINE AND WAS BORN IN PALESTINE.

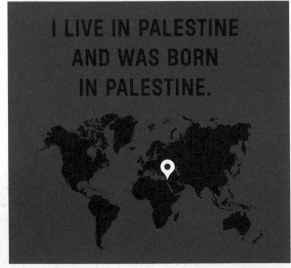

When I was 6, there was a cartoon about the future that I used to watch. I was amazed by the technology in it. I remember telling my father about the future of technology and he encouraged me to be curious. I eventually studied computer science. Now that I am older and wiser, whenever I meet someone younger who is following their studies I like to pass on all the helpful knowledge I can to help them.

ZDRAVO! MY NAME IS DARKO.

I AM **38** YEARS OLD.

I LIVE IN THE USA AND WAS BORN IN MACEDONIA.

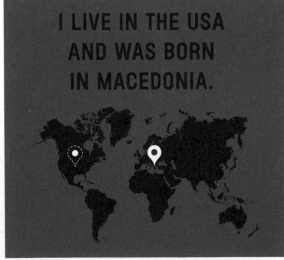

I was born left-handed. I used my left hand for writing and drawing, but I used my right hand for other things, like throwing balls. With a little practice over time, I worked out how to write with both hands. It was very useful, especially when I hurt my left shoulder in a sports game just before a big test! I still use both hands. When my left hand gets tired, I use my right. Just a few weeks ago, I used my skills for an important exam!

YA SOU! MY NAME IS CONSTANTINE.

I AM **39** YEARS OLD.

I LIVE IN THE USA AND WAS BORN IN GREECE.

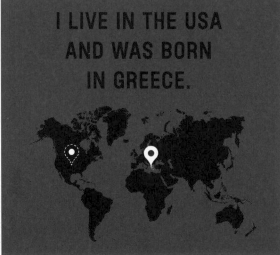

I like thinking of each year of my life as a point. One year = 1 point. I spent 18 points growing up in Athens in Greece, dreaming of America's New York City. I spent five points studying at school for something I didn't like, four points being married, two points writing a book, and two points learning how to make movies, which is what I love! All those points make me who I am. I make films now, and I love to tell stories that inspire people to use their points for what they truly love.

¡HOLA! MY NAME IS SEBASTIÁN.

I AM **40** YEARS OLD.

I LIVE IN ARGENTINA AND WAS BORN IN ARGENTINA.

Ever since I was a child, I liked listening to and giving advice to others. When I was 11, I remember helping one of my teenage cousins who had a problem with someone he loved. We laughed a lot about my very serious advice as neither of us had any real experience with love! Now I am a therapist who helps people talk about their problems. It feels great to be 40. I still feel young, but I am more experienced and mature.

¡HOLA! MY NAME IS RUBÉN.

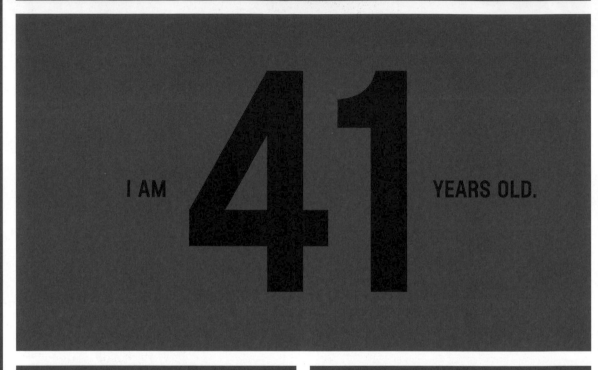

I AM **41** YEARS OLD.

I LIVE IN CHILE AND WAS BORN IN CHILE.

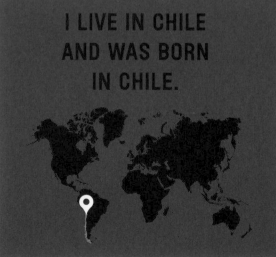

When I was 7 or 8, I played with a camera that my dad had. It was as big as a shoebox! There was no battery inside, so I never took any real photos. When I was a little older, my dad bought another camera, which I played with all the time, pretending to be a photographer. Years later, I am an audiovisual teacher. I teach people the best way to use a camera to make videos!

CZEŚĆ! MY NAME IS MARCIN.

I AM **42** YEARS OLD.

I LIVE IN POLAND AND WAS BORN IN POLAND.

I love my age. But age for me is just a number. What is most important is how you feel. Right now, I feel awesome! When I was a schoolboy, my grandmother once said: "Remember to always help other people and never expect anything in return." I thought this was a brilliant idea, so I've always helped others all my life. But I *do* get something in return: I help the world be a better place.

SALUT! MY NAME IS ANDRA.

I AM **43** YEARS OLD.

I LIVE IN SINGAPORE AND WAS BORN IN ROMANIA.

I was 7 when I began to ride a bike. One of my friends had a bike and a group of us took turns learning to ride it. As soon as someone fell off, the next kid took the bike. The bike was far too big for me and I couldn't stay on for more than ten seconds, but I was determined! One afternoon, after many falls and burning elbows and knees, I did it! Since that day, cycling has always made me happy.

¡HOLA! MY NAME IS AMADEO.

I AM **44** YEARS OLD.

I LIVE IN ARGENTINA AND WAS BORN IN BOLIVIA.

When I was 12, I wanted to learn how to drive, so I could help my father in the fields. He sold fruit and vegetables. I still drive to go to work. The most meaningful age for me was 18 because that's how old I was when I met my wife. We have been together for more than 25 years now and have three children together. Family is what is most important to me and what makes me happy. I am 44 and I feel good about it.

BONJOUR! MY NAME IS SANDRINE.

I AM **45** YEARS OLD.

I LIVE IN BELGIUM AND WAS BORN IN BELGIUM.

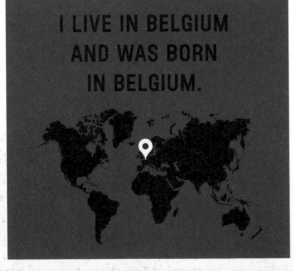

When I was 6, I used to pick strawberries in the woods with my grandfather and go home with a full basket. My grandmother used to tell me stories about her life during the Second World War. When she was 10 years old, she and her parents and little sister left her house, school, and friends behind, taking just a few clothes. They went to find peace. They lived with a French family who were willing to share the few things they had with them.

HELLO! MY NAME IS YOHANCE.

I AM **46** YEARS OLD.

I LIVE IN THE UNITED ARAB EMIRATES AND WAS BORN IN JAMAICA.

When I was 3, I always got into trouble for drawing with crayons and chalk on the walls outside my grandmother's house in Jamaica. But my family would quickly forgive me because they secretly liked them. I never stopped drawing, and I am an artist today. I remember when I turned 20, I thought my life would end because I was old! Looking back, I see how silly that was because I still feel as young today as when I was 20.

HALLO! MY NAME IS MERI.

I AM  **47** YEARS OLD.

I LIVE IN THE NETHERLANDS
AND WAS BORN
IN THE NETHERLANDS.

When I was a child, my brother and I spent a lot of time playing outside in nature. When I was 6, I started helping my grandfather with his fruit and vegetable garden. We planted carrots and cabbage as well as onions and beans. Picking strawberries was what I liked the most. Now my job is to take care of nature and carefully plan how we use the countryside. My two sons also love to spend time outside and this makes me really happy.

CHÀO BAN! MY NAME IS VU.

I AM **48** YEARS OLD.

I LIVE IN VIETNAM AND WAS BORN IN VIETNAM.

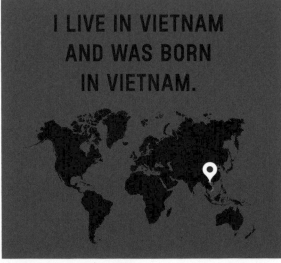

When I was a child, life was hard in Vietnam. Most of the family did not have enough food for each day, so having a toy was a real treat. When I was 3, my dream was to have a doll. My father left Vietnam around that time, to study in Bulgaria. Two years later, he sent me a big box for my 5th birthday. I opened it and I cried when I saw the doll inside. She was so cute!

SALAM! MY NAME IS WASIM.

I AM **49** YEARS OLD.

I LIVE IN THE USA AND WAS BORN IN PAKISTAN.

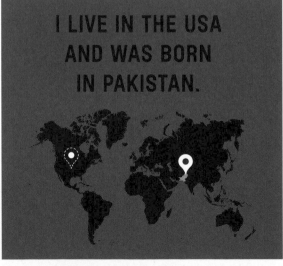

When I was 10, on Mother's Day, my brothers and I were trying to bake a cake and I accidentally started a fire! It burned our kitchen and caused a lot of damage. Later that day, I told my mother that I wanted to become a firefighter when I grew up. Years later, I completed my learning at the New York Fire Academy. I can't believe I am 49. That's crazy because next year I will be 50, and that's a big number!

HELLO! MY NAME IS KATE.

I AM  YEARS OLD.

50

I LIVE IN LUXEMBOURG AND WAS BORN IN THE UNITED KINGDOM.

I am someone who lives in the moment, so my best age is the one I am right now. I really don't feel as if I have finished growing up yet, and I'm pretty sure my kids would say that I haven't! When I was a child, 50 seemed impossibly old. But I don't feel old now! I have plenty of energy and a long list of things I want to do. The list grows longer every day!

¡HOLA! MY NAME IS JOSE.

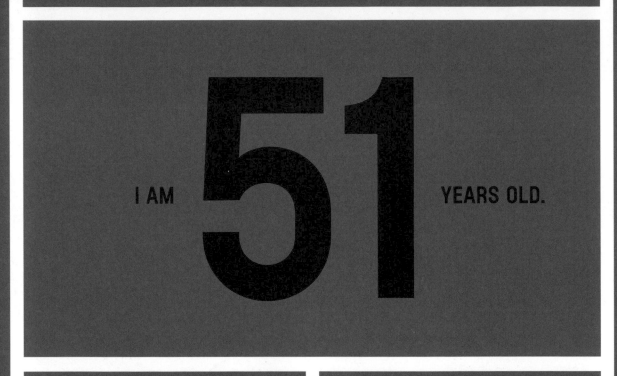

I AM **51** YEARS OLD.

I LIVE IN THE USA AND WAS BORN IN GUATEMALA.

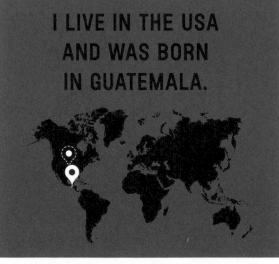

I was born in a little town called Siquinalá in Guatemala. When I was 10, I used to get up at five in the morning to pick cotton plants until seven at night, during school holidays. In the cotton fields, you tied a sack to your waist and picked as much cotton as you could. At the end of the day you weighed the sack at the station and you were paid three cents a pound. When I was 16 I moved to the United States for a better life.

HELLO! MY NAME IS SHAWN.

I AM **52** YEARS OLD.

I LIVE IN THE USA
AND WAS BORN IN
TRINIDAD AND TOBAGO.

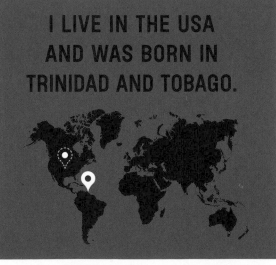

When I was 12, one of my jobs was to build all the fabulous background sets for our school plays and performances. It was a big deal. I was taught how to work with my hands, create art, build things, and make fun posters. Turning the school stage into a different world was magic for me. Today I have a very different job working with money, but thanks to my teachers at school, I have many of the skills I need in life.

¡HOLA! MY NAME IS SONIA.

I AM **53** YEARS OLD.

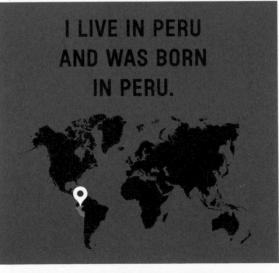

I LIVE IN PERU AND WAS BORN IN PERU.

When I was a child, I dreamed of having many children and being a teacher. I have always wanted to help children realize their dreams. I made those wishes come true, but I had lots of other dreams too! Because I have met many people who have taught me great lessons in my life, I felt it was my turn to tell stories and teach. So I became an artist! Best of all, I still have a lot more to learn and to dream about!

NAMASKĀRA! MY NAME IS BAL.

I AM **54** YEARS OLD.

I LIVE IN THE USA AND WAS BORN IN NEPAL.

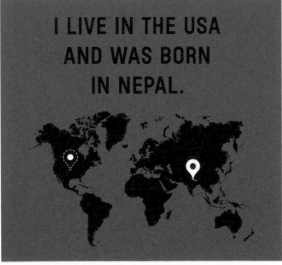

I grew up with a dad who had disabilities. I remember always thinking about how to fix his problems. I wanted to give him everything I could. Because my dad could no longer work, I left Nepal in search of work when I was 9. My last memory with my dad is when I was 16 and we were drinking a lot of tea together. Nothing is more important to me than family, and I want everyone to learn about where their parents and older family come from.

¡HOLA! MY NAME IS MARGARITA.

I AM  **55** YEARS OLD.

I LIVE IN THE DOMINICAN REPUBLIC AND WAS BORN IN THE DOMINICAN REPUBLIC.

When I was a little girl, I lived in many places. My father was an ambassador who helped other countries work with and understand our country. When I was 17, I spent my time teaching adults to read and write. That's how I knew I wanted to help people find what they need to learn. Today I am the director of a school for young children. Seeing my students do well makes me really happy.

¡HOLA! MY NAME IS MARCO.

I AM **56** YEARS OLD.

I LIVE IN NICARAGUA AND WAS BORN IN NICARAGUA.

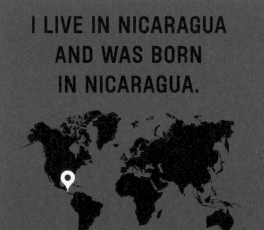

It's okay to not know what you want to do when you grow up. It's something that you often discover as you get older. I knew what I wanted to do when I was 15: to have my own business and to study engineering, so that I could build my own buildings! I finished college when I was 24 and, when I was 33, I built my first office building. Since then, I have built six other office buildings that I rent out to businesses in Managua, Nicaragua.

SALAM! MY NAME IS SAFARINA.

I AM  57 YEARS OLD.

I LIVE IN INDONESIA AND WAS BORN IN INDONESIA.

It doesn't matter how old I am, I always look forward to my next birthday. At 27 I got married, at 28 I had my first baby girl, and at 38 I had my baby boy and finished my studies, so all of those ages mean a lot to me. I am a scientist now, but before that I was a veterinarian, helping animals. I really like working as a scientist because it is exciting and unique. My family, my work, and music make me happy in life.

MONI! MY NAME IS ANNA.

I AM **58** YEARS OLD.

I LIVE IN MALAWI AND WAS BORN IN MALAWI.

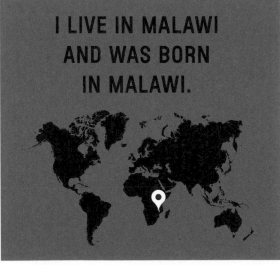

When I was young, I thought anyone who was 58 years old was a very old person! Now that I'm 58, I don't think that way anymore. I feel young and full of energy. My parents valued education and they made sure I thought it was important too. It gave me the chance to have an exciting and satisfying life! I set up a school called Mzuzu International Academy, and it makes me so happy when I see our students succeed.

HELLO! MY NAME IS AUDREY.

I AM  **59** YEARS OLD.

I LIVE IN SCOTLAND AND WAS BORN IN SCOTLAND.

I remember a very special teacher I used to have when I was 7. Her name was Mrs. Gillespie. She was a wonderful teacher who cared for her students, created exciting lessons, and was very kind to us. She made it my dream to become a teacher. So I worked hard at school and college to get to my goal. It is a job I have now been doing for 40 years and I have loved every day of it.

I AM  60 YEARS OLD.

I LIVE IN TANZANIA AND WAS BORN IN TANZANIA.

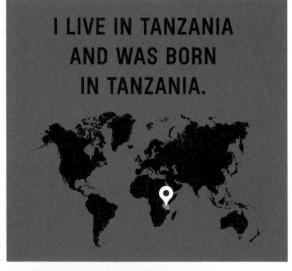

When I was a child, my dream was to become a teacher. I asked my father if I could go to school. He said it was more important to take care of his cows in order to feed the family, so I didn't go. When I had my own children, I made sure that they went to school, so they could follow their dreams. I want to keep working as a farmer, but it's hard work. I'm thinking of doing work that is easier for my body, like raising chickens and selling their eggs.

SAIBAIDEE! MY NAME IS KHAMPHANH.

I AM **61** YEARS OLD.

I LIVE IN FRANCE AND WAS BORN IN LAOS.

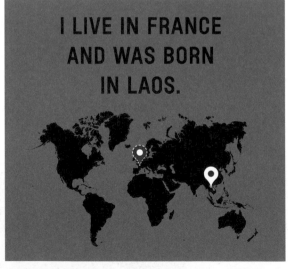

I grew up in Savannakhet in Laos. I remember the Vietnamese New Year celebrations we used to have when I as a child. New Year's Eve was special to me. I would spend the day at my grandparents' house cleaning it from top to bottom. It's Vietnamese tradition to remove all the dust and any bad luck and evil spirits before welcoming in the new year. I would go back home tired, but happy and dream of the week of celebrations and treats ahead.

¡HOLA! MY NAME IS RODRIGO.

I AM 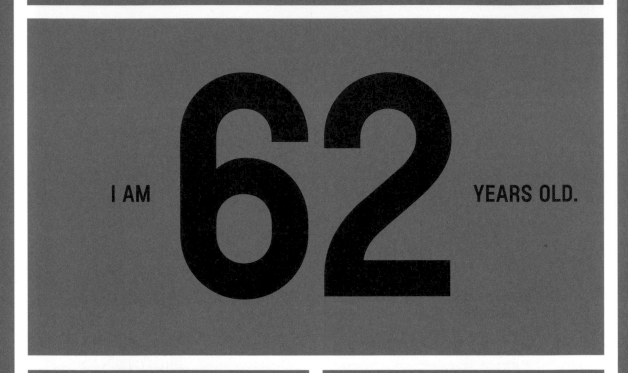 62 YEARS OLD.

I LIVE IN VENEZUELA AND WAS BORN IN VENEZUELA.

Being 62 is very pleasant thanks to the experiences I've gained over all my years. I grew up in a beautiful country with my parents and brother, in a home full of love, rules, and values. I was surrounded by all my family. The best things in my life are my loved ones. They have such a huge place in my heart. My work as an artist is also very important to me as it allows me to show my inner world to others.

ZDRAVO! MY NAME IS ISMET.

I AM **63** YEARS OLD.

I LIVE IN BOSNIA AND HERZEGOVINA AND WAS BORN THERE TOO.

When I was young, I used to spend my summers with my grandfather in the countryside. I rode my horse, ran through the meadow, climbed trees, picked flowers, and washed myself in a stream of fresh mountain water. One day our sheep had gone into someone else's field. The owner got really angry and chased us with a stick. It was scary. That's the day I decided I wanted to be a quiet, peaceful man like my grandfather.

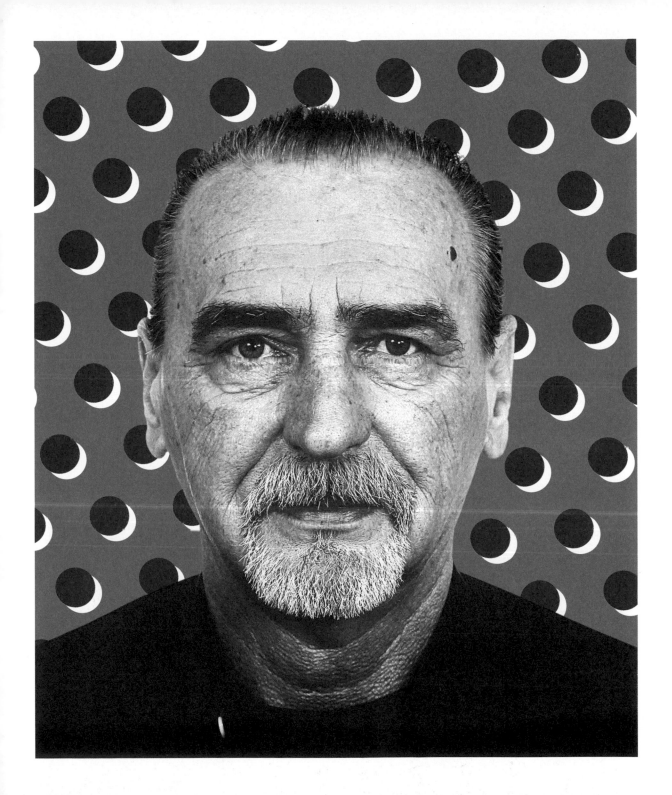

BONZOUR! MY NAME IS MALA.

I AM  **64** YEARS OLD.

I LIVE IN MAURITIUS AND WAS BORN IN MAURITIUS.

My mother was a dressmaker and used to make us beautiful dresses. I always liked clothes and I used to like watching the way people were dressed in movies from India. Later I worked in hotels, where looking good and speaking well are very important. I was happy to be doing something I liked. Even later, I started to teach students how to work in hotels and restaurants. Spending enough time with my family and my work is really important to me.

SALAM! MY NAME IS ZIAI.

I AM **65** YEARS OLD.

I LIVE IN FRANCE AND WAS BORN IN AFGHANISTAN.

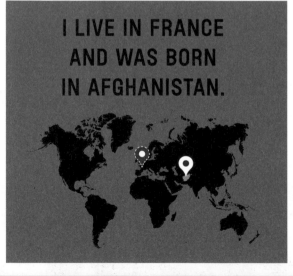

When I was 4, I had a picture book I loved, which was full of colors. One picture was of a bird's nest in a tree. Inside the nest, there were some baby birds. As I looked closer at the picture I started to worry because the tree didn't look strong enough to hold the nest! So I took a pencil and drew some branches on the tree to help. Now I design and build bridges!

SALAM! MY NAME IS MARYSE.

I AM **66** YEARS OLD.

I LIVE IN FRANCE AND WAS BORN IN TUNISIA.

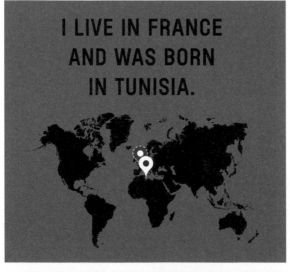

I grew up in Tunisia, which used to be a country where all lived together and had respect for one another. But things became harder. When I was 16, my father died, and some people made it hard for me to live in my own country. I had to leave. I came to France, where I had the chance to study and choose a job where I could help others. I trust you, and all the kids in the world, to build a better world together.

I AM  **67** YEARS OLD.

I LIVE IN GERMANY
AND WAS BORN
IN GERMANY.

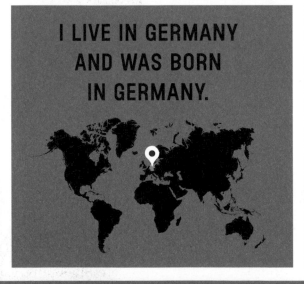

When I was 6, I went to a small stream near my parents' house with two friends. We managed to catch three trout with a butterfly net by chasing the fish into the net. We proudly went home with our trout and a damaged net. My mother was surprised but also a little bit angry with me. She made us put the trout back in the stream instead of cooking them. I feel that every age gives me special chances, so I love them all.

HALLÓ! MY NAME IS FINNBOGI.

I AM **68** YEARS OLD.

I LIVE IN ICELAND AND WAS BORN IN ICELAND.

When I was 10, during the winter the city was full of snow and I used to build snowmen and snow houses and go everywhere on a sled. Where I live, we only have four to five hours of daylight in the winter, but during the summer, the sun doesn't set! It is light all day and all night. I used to go everywhere on a bicycle, play ball games, and build huts and small cars I could sit in and ride. Now I am the happiest grandfather of nine grandchildren.

ANNYEONG HASEYO! MY NAME IS YOUNGSIK.

I AM **69** YEARS OLD.

I LIVE IN SOUTH KOREA AND WAS BORN IN SOUTH KOREA.

When I was 7, I used to get sick easily. I was often at the doctor's in my little town. Our doctor had snow-white hair and always had a smile on his face. He would whisper, "You will feel better soon" to me. They sounded like magic words. I never met my grandfather because he died before I was born, but this doctor made me think of him. Later I became a neurosurgeon, a doctor for people's heads, so I could help people too.

SHALOM! MY NAME IS ILANA.

I AM **70** YEARS OLD.

I LIVE IN ISRAEL AND WAS BORN IN ISRAEL.

I am very proud of my age. I don't feel like an old person. I feel like a person with a lot of experience that I can use to help others. I worked in a home for older people for many years. Now I visit older people who want company because sometimes they don't have many friends or family near them and can be very lonely. I hope for a world where people will take care of each other and look after those who are lonely.

¡HOLA! MY NAME IS JOSÉ.

I AM  **71** YEARS OLD.

I LIVE IN EL SALVADOR AND WAS BORN IN EL SALVADOR.

When I was 22, I decided to become a farmer. Seeing water in rivers, animals in the field, and crops like corn growing made me very happy. This is why I thought that being a farmer would be a good life for me. I feel happy about my age because I've seen my children grow and make their own families. I feel a little sad about my next birthday because my wife died a few years ago and I can't celebrate it with her. But I'm happy to be surrounded by my family.

PËRSHËNDETJE! MY NAME IS SABRIJE.

I AM  **72** YEARS OLD.

I LIVE IN KOSOVO AND WAS BORN IN KOSOVO.

I did not think I would live longer than my children. I lost two sons in the Kosovo-Serbia war in 1999. Thankfully, I now have a home with my other son and my daughters, and 14 loving grandchildren. They all make me feel happy and like my life is full.

AHOJ! MY NAME IS JELA.

I AM  **73** YEARS OLD.

I LIVE IN THE CZECH REPUBLIC AND WAS BORN IN THE CZECH REPUBLIC.

I was a nurse my whole life. I used to work in a hospital and for people with disabilities. I took care of people in my family and in my area too. I like being there for people who need it. Being my age is not always easy – I have arthrosis, which makes my fingers hurt. But I am very lucky to live close to my sons and grandchildren. I love them so much! I loved taking care of them and now they take care of me too.

SALAM! MY NAME IS ABDERRAHMANE.

I AM **74** YEARS OLD.

I LIVE IN FRANCE AND WAS BORN IN ALGERIA.

When I was a child, I worked as a gardener in a city by the sea in Algeria during the holidays. It helped me make money and be near the sea. Now that I don't work, I spend my time gardening, and I love it. I think this love comes from my childhood summers. I am 74, but getting older is not scary to me. I have children and grandchildren who make me happy, and I love what I have now.

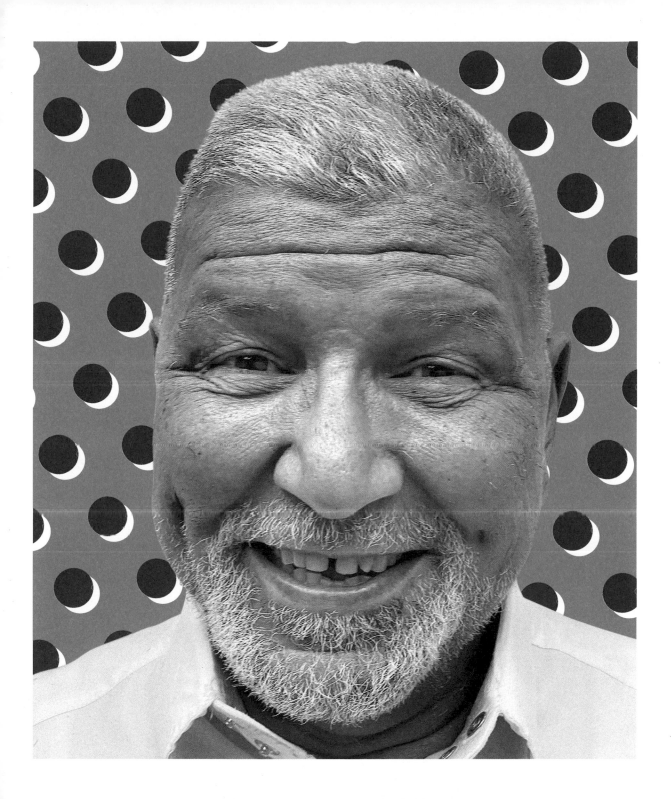

PËRSHËNDETJE! MY NAME IS NAXHIJE.

I AM **75** YEARS OLD.

I LIVE IN THE UNITED KINGDOM AND WAS BORN IN ALBANIA.

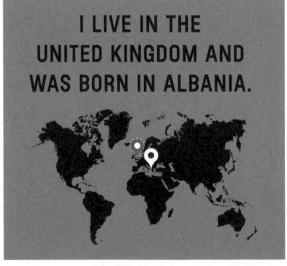

I was born at the end of the Second World War. There was destruction and poor people all around, and most people couldn't read or write. I had nine sisters and brothers. We gathered together every evening, after a tiring day. We were poor but happy. When I was 7, I started going to school. I was badly dressed and I didn't have shoes. I collected berries to make ink for my school pen. These problems didn't matter though — I wanted to go to school so much.

TENA KOUTOU! MY NAME IS ROD.

I AM **76** YEARS OLD.

I LIVE IN THE UNITED KINGDOM AND WAS BORN IN NEW ZEALAND.

I was born during the Second World War. There were lots of cows nearby, but nearly all the milk and butter was sent to Britain to feed the army and people. I wish for a more peaceful world now. When I was 8, I read one or two books a week. Now I think I've read more than 7,000 books in my life! I love meeting people, so I became a church minister. I've led hundreds of marriages and other important meetings at the church. I still love meeting people!

SALAM! MY NAME IS MAMANDINE.

I AM **77** YEARS OLD.

I LIVE IN GAMBIA AND WAS BORN IN GAMBIA.

I got married when I was 20, and I raised my children until my 50s. I am a farmer, but I am also the "Alkalo," which means I'm the leader of my village. I am really proud to see our local school get better, with clean water and electricity. It's called the Lamin Koto super-school. I am looking forward to my 80s and 90s because I will get to see my grandchildren become adults. I wish for world peace.

LÍ HÓ-BÒ! MY NAME IS FRANK.

I AM **78** YEARS OLD.

I LIVE IN AUSTRALIA AND WAS BORN IN TAIWAN.

I grew up in an old-style house in a village in Taiwan. It didn't have running water, so my brothers and sister and I used to carry home buckets of water with a bamboo stick on our shoulders from the stream. When I was 34, I created my own architecture business – designing and planning new and different buildings. When I was 45, I moved to Australia with my family. I worked very hard to be my own person and have a very different life from my childhood.

ZDRAVO! MY NAME IS RAFAEL.

I AM  YEARS OLD.

I LIVE IN SLOVENIA AND WAS BORN IN SLOVENIA.

I started going to school when I was 7. Our school was small, old, and made of wood. We didn't have heating or toilets, and the teachers were very strict. But home was a warm place. I had my parents and my siblings and a cherry tree that was my hideaway. I used to do my homework and studying in my tree. Later I moved to the city and learned to fix and make electrical tools and equipment. I am really proud of my job, and even at my age, I still work.

HELLO! MY NAME IS ANNE.

I AM **80** YEARS OLD.

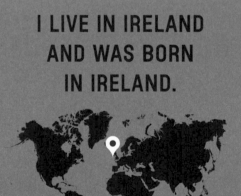

I LIVE IN IRELAND AND WAS BORN IN IRELAND.

When I was a little girl I played from morning to night with my four sisters and two brothers. But when I was 6, my older sister became sick and died. It was a really hard time for my parents, so I stayed with my aunt and uncle. I kept very busy feeding their hens and ducks and collecting slugs and snails, but I missed my family. I will never forget the day I went back home. I felt so loved and so happy to be with my family again.

HELLO! MY NAME IS DOROTHY.

I AM **81** YEARS OLD.

I LIVE IN CANADA AND WAS BORN IN CANADA.

I was a waitress for 35 years, but now I'm retired, which means I no longer work. I'm very happy in my 80s because I can do what I want. When I was younger I couldn't say no to anything, but now I don't have any trouble saying no! What makes me happiest is the calmness and peace that comes with age. I had a great relationship with my grandfather. He once told me that grandparents are there to love their grandchildren. I agree with him.

¡HOLA! MY NAME IS ANTONIO.

I AM **82** YEARS OLD.

I LIVE IN PUERTO RICO AND WAS BORN IN PUERTO RICO.

When I was a kid, I spent a lot of time with my grandfather. He always made me feel special. I helped him with small chores and writing letters. He would take me around town on his horse and pay me five cents, so that I could buy coconut ice. My favorite age is when I was 16. I went to the United States for the first time, and I played baseball with my friends every day. Sometimes I feel old, but I still have many hopes and dreams!

I AM  **83** YEARS OLD.

I LIVE IN UKRAINE AND WAS BORN IN UKRAINE.

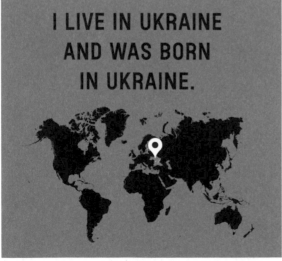

When I was 9, my parents died. My brother and sister and I moved in with family friends in a small town. I used to work with farm animals and vegetables to earn money. It was hard work, but taking care of my family is the most important thing in the world. One day, I came home with warm bread, cheese, and a pie. My brother and sister were so excited! I feel happy and lucky to be 83 years young. I even have great-grandchildren.

ZDRAVO! MY NAME IS JOKA.

I AM **84** YEARS OLD.

I LIVE IN SERBIA AND WAS BORN IN SERBIA.

When I was 4 years old, the Second World War started. Life was really tough, but I always thought of the future and believed I could do anything. I wasn't allowed to go to school because I was a girl, which didn't make sense to me. But thanks to my brother's help, I learned how to read and write. I made sure my children went to school. I am very proud of them! Now I have six grandchildren and nothing is hard anymore. I love being old with family.

¡HOLA! MY NAME IS YVETTE.

I AM **85** YEARS OLD.

I LIVE IN FRANCE AND WAS BORN IN COLOMBIA.

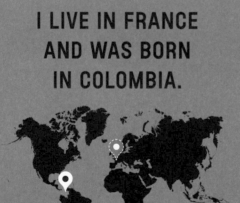

When I was 15, I had the chance to help a doctor who gave free visits to people in my small fishing village in Colombia. That's how I realized how wonderful it was to give to others. I've carried on doing this my entire life, giving to my children, my grandchildren, and my work. I worked in a job that took care of older people in their homes. It is easy to give and giving is so fulfilling. Even a smile, or a nice word, can be worth a lot.

SALAM! MY NAME IS ESTHER.

I AM **86** YEARS OLD.

I LIVE IN FRANCE AND WAS BORN IN MOROCCO.

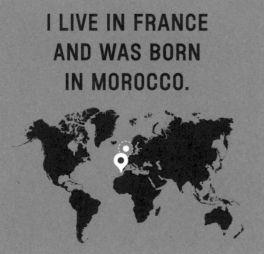

At 86, I am happy because I am still walking well. I am not worried about the future. The most important thing for me is for my children and grandchildren to be healthy and well. I want to spend my last good years having beautiful moments with them because that is what truly makes me happy.

¡HOLA! MY NAME IS TERESA.

I AM  **87** YEARS OLD.

I LIVE IN ARGENTINA AND WAS BORN IN SPAIN.

I feel great about my age. I feel as if I am 20 years old! The most important age for me was 21 because that's when I gave birth to my only child. I wish for a peaceful world and that we could all live together as one.

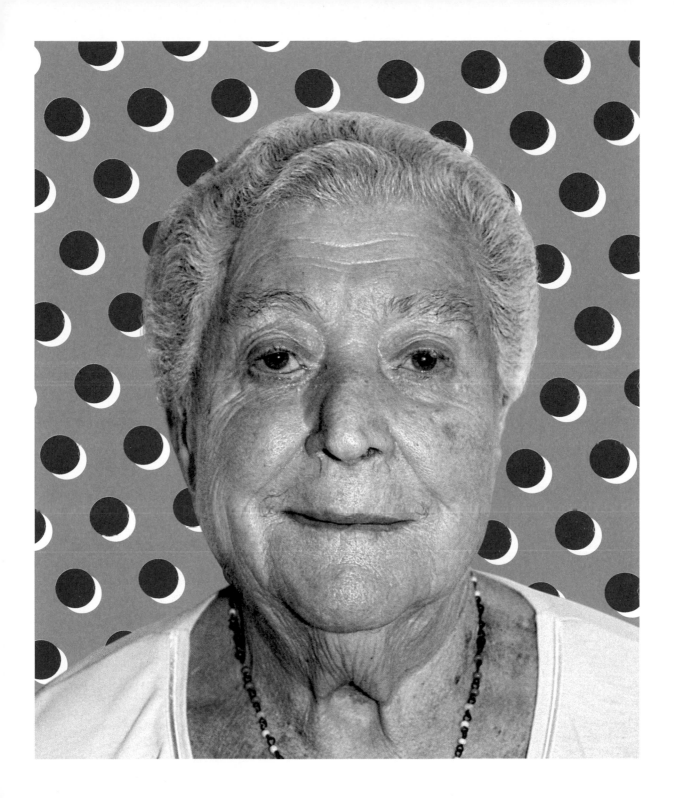

SALEMETSIN BE! MY NAME IS KHAKIM.

I AM  88 YEARS OLD.

I LIVE IN KAZAKHSTAN AND WAS BORN IN KAZAKHSTAN.

When I was 10, a war broke out and my father went to fight. I had to start working at a glass factory as well as the local grocery store. Because my father was a math teacher, he had taught me to count quickly, which helped for the store! Because I didn't get enough to eat when I was a child, I'm not very healthy now. Today my family is what makes me happiest, but I also like playing a good game of chess.

HELLÓ! MY NAME IS TESSA.

I AM **89** YEARS OLD.

I LIVE IN AUSTRALIA AND WAS BORN IN HUNGARY.

I was a child during the Second World War. When I was 13 we would hide in an air-raid shelter if there were falling bombs. When I was a teenager, the city I lived in had been destroyed by bombs. I think that living through war made me stronger and ready for the harder things in life. I still feel young inside. My family is the most important thing to me. I am really excited because I am going to be a great-grandmother soon!

ASSALAM-O-ALAIKUM! MY NAME IS MENASHE.

I AM

90

YEARS OLD.

I LIVE IN CANADA AND WAS BORN IN IRAQ.

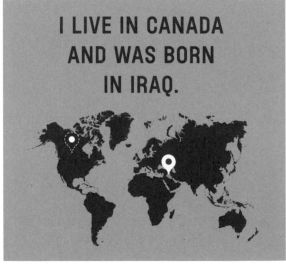

When I was 21, I moved to Israel because life wasn't very safe in Iraq. I lived and worked on a farm where I was taught to work hard and make my own food and money. I still love gardening. When I was 13 and still lived in Iraq, I was unable to have my Bar Mitzvah, a special celebration for Jewish boys of that age. But my family decided to have one for me when I was 89! It shows it's never too late to achieve your goals in life.

¡HOLA! MY NAME IS DOMINGA.

I AM **91** YEARS OLD.

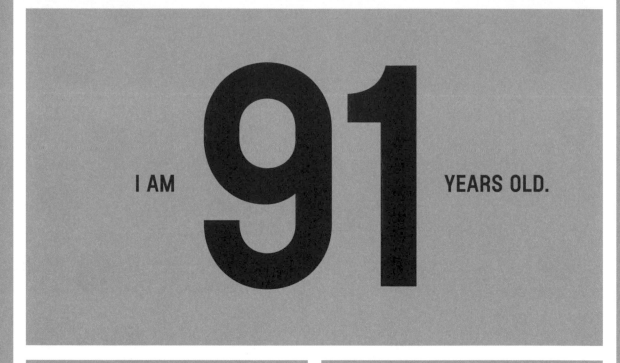

I LIVE IN THE DOMINICAN REPUBLIC AND WAS BORN IN CUBA.

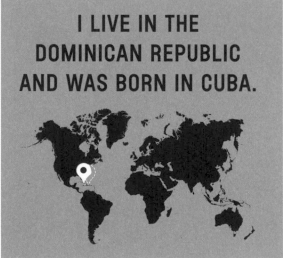

I am the third of ten brothers and sisters. When I was 12, I had to leave school to help at home. I was very sad, especially to miss my math class that I loved. But family was more important. Later I had two kids who needed special attention because they were hard of hearing. I moved to the city and got a job as a teacher's assistant, so that they could go to school and have a good life. Now I enjoy seeing my great-granddaughters go to college.

LUMELA! MY NAME IS MANYAKALLO.

I AM **92** YEARS OLD.

I LIVE IN LESOTHO AND WAS BORN IN LESOTHO.

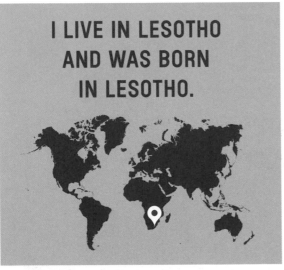

My twin sister and I used to play netball, which is like basketball but without bouncing the ball! We had a lot of fun switching roles during matches without anyone noticing! When I was 8, I would pick and sell peaches in the village to make money to buy candy. In my 50s, I followed my dream and started my own business selling potato chips and peanuts. I still do this. I am looking forward to my next birthday because my family has promised me a big party!

SAWASDEE! MY NAME IS AM-ON.

I AM  YEARS OLD.

93

I LIVE IN THAILAND AND WAS BORN IN THAILAND.

I feel very blessed to have lived a long life doing what I love. I helped to sell cars around the world and have lots of good memories from that! I really enjoyed learning new things from different cultures and places. Age doesn't matter to me, but I wish for good health and love from family and friends. I love it when my children and grandchildren come to visit. I wish for the world to be filled with love and peace everywhere.

OLÁ! MY NAME IS AYA.

I AM **94** YEARS OLD.

I LIVE IN BRAZIL AND WAS BORN IN BRAZIL.

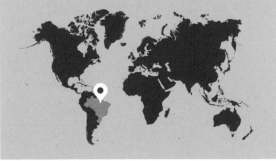

My parents moved from Japan to Brazil to farm coffee bean plants. My best memories are from when I was a child. I always looked forward to my parents carrying me on their back while they worked in the coffee fields. A couple of years ago, I was in a car accident. I have to use a wheelchair to get around now. But I've loved every year of my life and want to live it to the fullest.

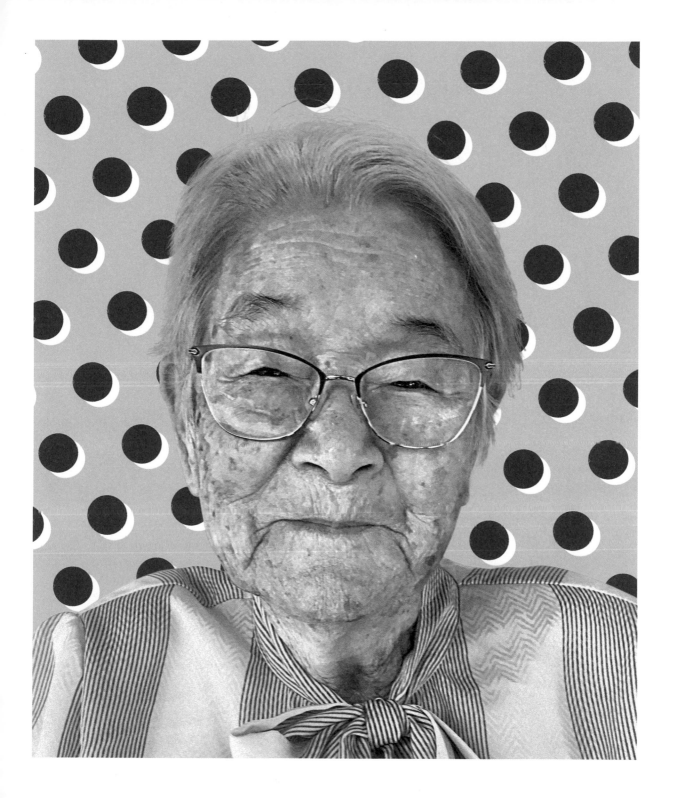

GAMARJOBA! MY NAME IS MARIKA.

I AM **95** YEARS OLD.

I LIVE IN GEORGIA AND WAS BORN IN GEORGIA.

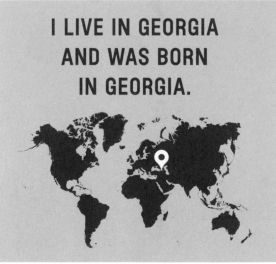

When I was 5, I caught a disease. In my culture, people believe diseases don't go away until a child's wish comes true. I wanted Mrs. Ermonia, the tailor who made clothes, to visit me. Everyone was surprised by my strange wish except for my mother. She knew I wanted to sew dresses for my dolls. My parents contacted her and got some cloth for me. I was so happy, the disease went away! I still enjoy sewing the most.

MERHABA! MY NAME IS HASAN.

I AM  **96** YEARS OLD.

I LIVE IN TURKEY AND WAS BORN IN TURKEY.

I had a big family of 43 people! We lived together in a two-bedroom house in a very small village, but we were very happy. There was no pharmacy in our village, so when we got sick, we drank a mixture of boiled yogurt and red pepper. It was the best medicine! I got married and moved to a bigger village when I was 30. I worked at the railway station until my 70s. I have nine children and 45 grandchildren. Now I live with my family in an apartment.

KONNICHIWA! MY NAME IS MASAKO.

I AM **97** YEARS OLD.

I LIVE IN JAPAN AND WAS BORN IN JAPAN.

I can't believe my own age: 97! Wow! That's old! What have I been doing all this time? I actually lived through the Second World War. It was a terrible time. But I feel lucky to now live in a time where we are free to try anything we want. Having something you want to do is the best thing in the world. My wish is for all the children of the world to try all kinds of things. There is so much you can do. Go for it! I'm cheering for you.

OLÁ! MY NAME IS ALCIDES.

I AM  98 YEARS OLD.

I LIVE IN PORTUGAL AND WAS BORN IN PORTUGAL.

My childhood was not easy as my mother died when I was 7. I had to work hard. I left my village to work on a farm nearby, looking after sheep. When I was 10, I moved and worked on another farm for many years until I could buy my own land. When I was a boy there were no fancy farming machines. I worked the land by hand. Now I miss working on the land. I was also a hunter and a fisherman in the early morning. I want to be 100. I only have a little more to go!

¡HOLA! MY NAME IS CARMEN.

I AM **99** YEARS OLD.

I LIVE IN ECUADOR AND WAS BORN IN ECUADOR.

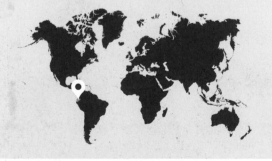

I had a very happy childhood, surrounded by family and friends. We played together a lot and had many parties and get-togethers as well as walks in the countryside. I had a big doll collection and I liked making my doll's dresses. Later in life, my daughter made clothes for me! Pretty silk dresses and suits. She knew what I liked and I used to dress well. I still have a happy life today, with my children, grandchildren, and great-grandchildren!

HELLO! MY NAME IS BEATRICE.

I AM  YEARS OLD.

I LIVE IN THE USA AND WAS BORN IN THE USA.

I was a sickly child with a heart problem, and I was allergic to everything, which meant I wasn't able to run around. When I was 7, I found the local library. I still love to read, and for the last ten years I have been a library volunteer. I never dreamed to be this age. It's an amazing experience. I am healthy and well, I don't walk with a cane, and I live alone. That's not common at my age and something to be grateful for.

HOW OLD DO YOU WANT TO BE?

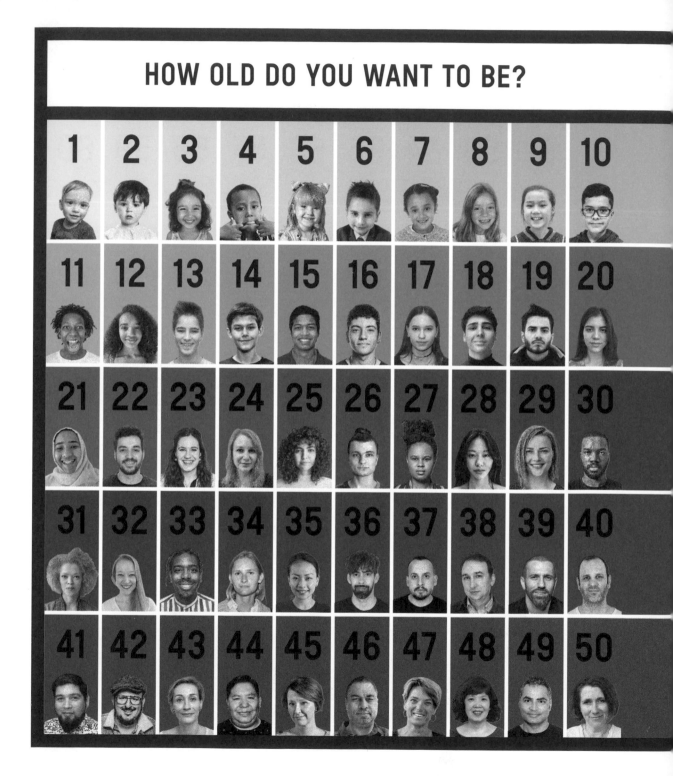

WHAT DO YOU WANT TO BE WHEN YOU GROW UP?

WHERE WERE
YOU BORN?
WHERE DO
YOU LIVE?

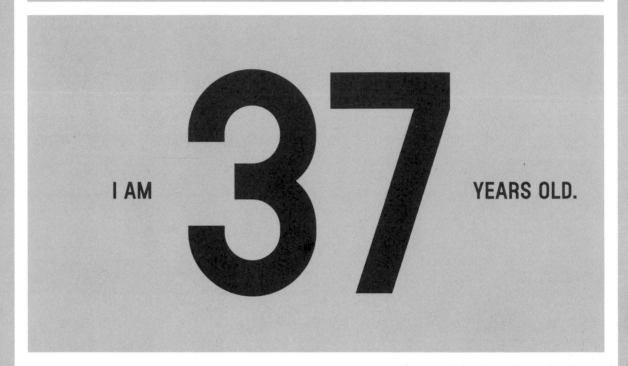

BONJOUR! MY NAME IS JR.

I AM **37** YEARS OLD.

I live in France and was born in France. When I was 16, I found a camera in a subway station. I took photos of my friends with it. Then I decided to put these pictures on walls around the city. It was my first exhibition and I called it *Sidewalk Galleries*. When I was 21, I put up a huge picture of a person's face on a wall in the suburbs of Paris. Soon I was taking pictures of people all around the world, printing them onto huge sheets of paper and then pasting them onto the walls of all kinds of cities! Walls and streets are the perfect place to show art because then everyone gets to see them. It's also a great way for the people in my pictures to share their stories – their memories, their experiences, and the things that are important to them. When I was 28, I won the famous TED prize, for my art. It helped me start the Inside Out Project, which is working to change the world. It's my dream come true.

THE INSIDE OUT PROJECT

The people and stories in this book are part of an art project called Inside Out. Inspired by the way the artist JR puts large black-and-white photos of people on buildings across the world, the Inside Out Project asks anyone from anywhere to send in pictures of their face. The photos are turned into large posters and sent back to those people, so that they can create art shows in their own cities or villages.

When we look at a large picture of a person's face, we may wonder who they are, what they do, and what stories they have to tell. Every person has their own story, and this project gives everyone the chance to share details of their lives and what they believe in.

The Inside Out Project has traveled all over the world, inspiring groups of people to talk about hope, how everyone is unique and should be allowed to be themselves, ways to stop people from hurting each other and having wars, how to help the Earth's plants and animals, and learning.

JR believes that art can change the world because it can spark conversations. Talking to each other can change the way we see other people. It can help us get along and help the world.

So far, more than 400,000 people from 142 countries have joined the Inside Out Project. *You* can too! Take a look at www.insideoutproject.net for more information.

I WISH FOR YOU
TO STAND UP FOR
WHAT YOU CARE ABOUT
BY PARTICIPATING IN
A GLOBAL ART PROJECT,
AND TOGETHER
WE'LL TURN THE WORLD....
INSIDE OUT
—JR

AN INSIDE OUT PROJECT IN GERMANY

AN INSIDE OUT PROJECT IN MALAWI

AN INSIDE OUT PROJECT AT THE NORTH POLE

AN INSIDE OUT PROJECT IN CANADA

AN INSIDE OUT PROJECT IN BANGLADESH

AN INSIDE OUT PROJECT IN EL SALVADOR

This project was made possible by Ludmila Kreichman from the Inside Out Project.

Special thanks to the JR studio: Marc Azoulay, Marc Berrebi, Camille Pajot, Quentin Besnard, Melvyn Bonnaffé, Mauve Chalandon, Marion Charlot, Valentin Crépain, Camille Garnier, Louis Joubert, Maud Malfettes, Luana Saltiel, Jaime Scatena, Emma Berrebi, Damariz Damken, Manon Ecotière, Natalia Espinoza, Emile Herlemont, and Lucas Scherrer

Special thanks also to Charlotte Urgese, Jean-François Rial, Jo Allan, Nathalie Belloir, Voyageurs du Monde, Fabrice Dabouineau, Anne Dumesnil, Michèle Mergui, Cécile Attal, Ariel Kliegerman, Matej Gal Pintar, Ales Josifovski, Philipp Engelhorn, Oliver Jeffers, Guillaume Sautier, Laurent Dusonchet, Margaux Fertat, Eric Deberdt, Selim Varol, Galerie Perrotin, Galleria Continua, Galerie Danysz, Esmé Lux, Olivier Barthelmé, Cecilia Pereira-Bahia, Nina Soutoul, Katie Swinden, Alastair Siddons, Seda Kalyoncu, Loïc Pugeat, Linda Schramm, Greg Yurra, Kuralai Abdukhalikova, Jona Shehu, Mads Tolstrup, Noémie Pugeat, Etan Pugeat, Prune Nourry, Elsa, Maryse, and Gerard

PHOTO CREDITS

A. Natirtsiksly, Abderrahmane Selami, Airy Toral, Aiuto Markus, Alayna Davidson, Alicia Herbert, Anna Parkinson, Anna Poncet, Anne & Christophe Mathieu, Anousonne Savanchomkeo, Antonio Cotto, Azra Heric, Bao Mengqi, Branko Lenadeia, Catherine Surany, Celine Darsa, Chiara Shehu, Christian Duval, Daniel Fuentealba, Daniel Rolider, Daniela Basse, Dario Inverizzi, Debarshi Sarkar, Deniz Taşdemir, Dondro, Doszhanov, Eleazar Parra, Elizabeth, Esther Azoulay, Finnbogi Helgason, Gabriela Orlowska, Gif Jittiwutikarn, Gil Eany, Gilda Jerez, Grace Chan, Gregory Lurra, Hailen Evjen, Heidi Lender, Hideo Torii, Hui-Wen Chang, Iain Lindsay, Jan Van Koekel, Jela Sigmundova, Jelena Danilovic, Jenssy Abigail Santos Santamaria, Jo Allan, John Keys, Kalle Lehto, Katie Anderson, Keshni Anupah Makoond, Kevin Akin-Abangwu, Kim Gronneberg, Laura Dergal, Le Ouang Dao, Lee Jin IL, Liridona Osmanaj, Luis Despradel, Luisina Aussel, M. Victoria Sananes, Malik Shaheen, Maria Joao Carralho, Mariane Ricaud, Marina Garcia Burgos, Mario Kreichman, Maryse Hania, Matin Bonakdar, Michaela Oppitz, Miguel Alvarez, Nathalie Gutenmacher, Ngondzashe Chinhara, Niki Kotsapouikin, Pamela Mongelos, Photo Pallak, Photo Team, Preeti Caberwal, Rafael Santiago Idrovo Espinoza, Saba Kakhadze, Salvador Carmona, Sandrine Brasseur, Sarah Ziai, Shawn N. West, Shawn Paul Tan, Slavyan Kostov, Snedden Monteiro, Sumayya Mohamed, Tahni Candelaria, Talia Saltiel, Thomas Tingström, Valdic Ceics, Vladimir Risteski, Walling McGarity LLC, X. Marle, Ylva Erevall, Yohance Douglas, Yoshiki Tsuji

PARTICIPANTS' NAMES

Abderrahmane Selami, Abedarahman Shurrab, Alcides Ferreira, Amaarah Garda, Amadeo Calla, Amira Mahilet Dergal, Am-On Wattanaporn, Anan Zhu, Andra Levy, Anna Msowoya Keys, Anne Parkinson, Antonio Cotto, Asmaa Abu Assaf, Audrey Lindsay, Aya Yuba, Bal Kishan Poudel Sharma, Beatrice Gold, Carmen Olimpia Polo Regalado, Constantine Venetopoulos, Daria Singer, Darko Dejanovski, Delfina Welwel, Diego Araya-Montero, Dominga Sixto Martinez, Dorothy Rodrigue, Elsa Frödel, Esther Bouhana, Esther Gatemba, Finnbogi Helgason, Francisco Porras, Frank Kuo Shong Jien, Grace Chan, Gwen Allan, Hasan Taşdemir, Ilana Shulman, Ismet Heric, Ivanka Brusilovska, Jela Sigmundova, Johnson Ricaud, Joka Balać, Jose Clara Santos, Jose Elmer Castellanos, Justin Lescanne, Kalle Lehto, Kate Loretto, Kevin Akin-Abangwu, Khakim Doszhanov, Khamphanh Savanchomkeo, Klaudia Lencz, Liam Bruno Pimentel Rodriguez, Liisi Sukles, Lorenzo Mier-y-Teran, Luka Alena Herbert, Mala Makoond, Mamandine Jabi, Manyakallo Lilly Shelile, Marcin Walencik, Marco Amador, Margarita Dargam, Maria Krupnovs, Mariam (Marika) Gvelesiani, Maryse Hania, Masako Fukami, Matin Bonakdar, Menashe Eany, Meri Loeffen, Michaela Oppitz, Mohamad Abdallah, Nadeilen Jezela Lopes Soares, Naxhije Hoxha, Ngonidzashe Chinhara, Noam Darsa, Olivia Zonetti, Oscar Pria, Pamela Mongelos, Rafael Lebar, Rania Caberwal, Rod Anderson, Rodrigo Ignacio Aguilar Parra, Ruben Alfredo Alarcon Valenzuela, Sabrije Osmanaj, Sacha Gutenmacher, Safarina G. Malik, Sahel Havran Manjarisoa Faed, Sandrine Brasseur, Sebastian Becker, Shawn J.P. West, Sheena Liam, Solveiga Kalva, Sonia Cunliffe, Teresa Consuelo Carballo de Fiores, Tessa Surany, Toma Nikolov, Vu Huong Giang, Walter Schramm, Wasim Husain, Yohance Douglas, Youngsik Kim, Yvette Nakache, Ziai Fahim

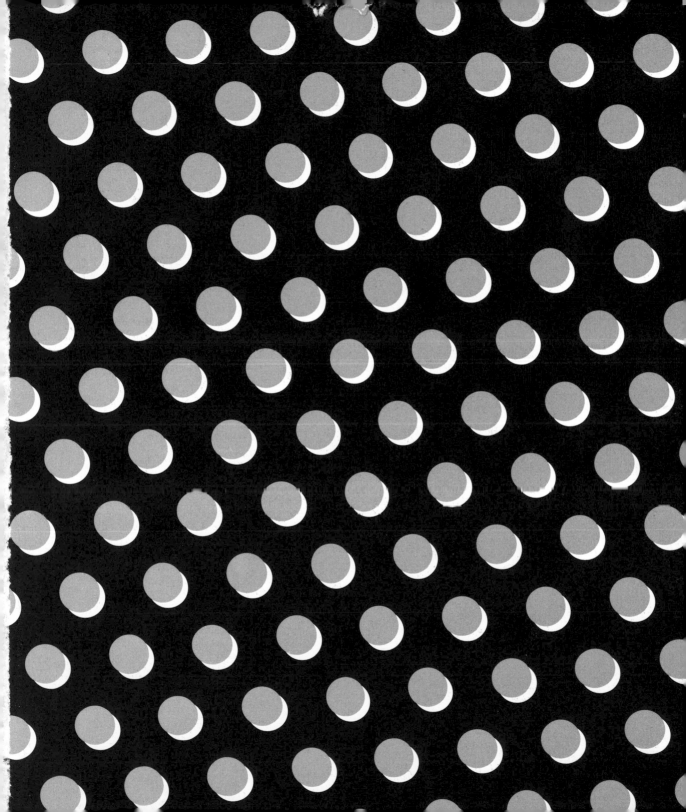

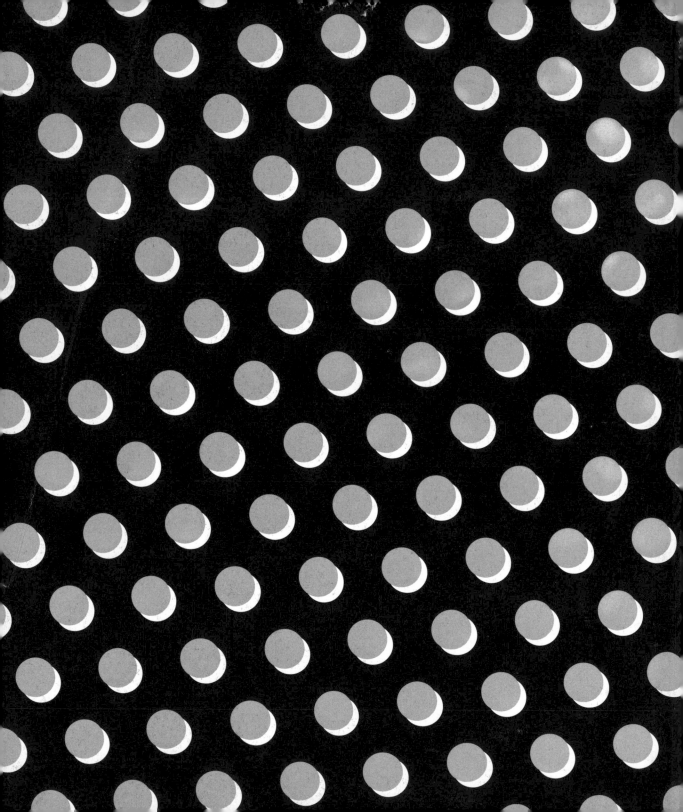